RELAT10NSHIP

Finding Relationship Through God's Top 10

RELAT1ØNSHIP

Finding Relationship Through God's Top 10

ROBERT MORRIS

STUDY GUIDE

CONTENTS

1

THE PRINCIPLE OF PRIORITY

The principle of priority is about putting God first in our lives When we honor Him with our firstfruits, He will always take care of us.

ENGAGE

What is your favorite springtime activity?

WATCH

Watch "The Principle of Priority."

- Look for the way God has established a relationship with His people.
- Consider ways to put God first in your life.

(If you are not able to watch this teaching on video, read the following. Otherwise, skip to the **Talk** section after viewing.)

READ

Last summer, I began to look at the Ten Commandments in a new way. I don't think God was giving us a list of rules. I think He was giving us a list of principles for living, and these principles enhance our relationship with Him and other people. The first commandment teaches us the principle of priority.

It's About Relationship

God is a God of relationship. He created Adam and Eve, redeemed the children of Israel, and redeemed you for relationship. In Exodus 20:1 He reminds Israel that He brought them out of slavery and bondage to have a relationship. Romans 6:6 says the same thing about us. When we see the Ten Commandments, we see principles of our relationship with God. *You* are the one who determines the depth of your relationship with God.

God gives the Ten Commandments in Exodus 20:3-17. Then in verses 18-21, we read:

> Now all the people witnessed the thunderings, the lightning flashes, the sound of the trumpet, and the mountain smoking; and when the people saw *it,* they trembled and stood afar off. Then they said to Moses, "You speak with us, and we will hear; but let not God speak with us, lest we die."
>
> And Moses said to the people, "Do not fear; for God has come to test you, and that His fear may be before you, so that you may

not sin." So the people stood afar off, but Moses drew near the thick darkness where God *was.*

Moses determined that he wanted to have a deeper relationship with God, but the people determined that they wanted to have a relationship with God through Moses. They asked Moses to speak to God and tell them what He said. How similar is that to the way Christians today want to hear from God through their pastor? The Israelites were afraid they would die. Yes, you do die when you enter the presence of God, but that is a great thing because then Jesus can live through you.

Psalm 103:7 says, "He made known His ways to Moses, / His acts to the children of Israel." Look at the difference. The children of Israel knew His acts; they knew *what* God did. Moses knew His ways—he knew *why* God did it. Moses understood the ways of God. He had a relationship based on the principles God taught in the commandments.

Worship God Only

Worship God only. This sums up the first commandment. Exodus 20:3 says, "You shall have no other gods before Me." This does not mean you can have some other gods *after* God. The word *before* is a preposition, and the phrase clarifies the simple statement that they shall have no other gods—period. Israel had just been in Egypt for 430 years. Egypt had more gods than any other society or culture. They had 29 main gods and more than 2,000 lesser gods. God was saying that you will have **no** other gods. The word translated *before* can also be translated as *besides me* or *other than me*. Isaiah 45:5 makes it clear: "I *am* the Lord, and *there is* no other; / *There is* no God besides Me." It is a principle of relationship.

This same principle is exhibited in marriage. One day many years ago, when God asked me to write down my priorities, He told me to write down "Debbie." I didn't understand at first, since I thought God should be number one. Then God said, "When you're married, if you'll put your spouse as number one, you are putting Me number one. Because if you can't serve her, you can't serve Me."

Put God First

Put God first is another way to describe this commandment and is a principle that runs all through Scripture. God told the Israelites to bring all the silver and gold from Jericho into His house, because Jericho was the first. He said to sacrifice the firstborn of their flocks—not just one of the first 10. It was the reason God accepted Abel's offering but not Cain's, and this was 2,500 years before the law and the Ten Commandments. God accepted Abel's offering because it was the firstfruits and rejected Cain's because it was not (see Exodus 4:3–5). Jesus reiterates this when He says in Matthew 6:33, "Seek first the kingdom of God and His righteousness, and all these things shall be added to you."

In 1 Kings 17:12–16, we see the same principle when the prophet Elijah goes to the widow in Zarephath, and she agrees to make a small cake of bread for him first. God then preserves her oil and flour, and it does not run out. Note that God's purpose was to provide for the widow as well as to provide for Elijah. She had one meal left, and God preserved her family when she put Him first. God will always take care of us when we put Him first.

NOTES

_____

_____

_____

_____

_____

_____

_____

_____

_____

_____

_____

_____

_____

TALK

These questions can be used for group discussion or personal reflection:

Question 1

How does tithing demonstrate that God is first in our lives?

_____

_____

_____

_____

Question 2

Read Psalm 103:7. What is the difference between knowing the *acts* of God and knowing the *ways* of God? What are some examples of His ways?

_____

_____

_____

_____

Question 3

Read 1 Kings 17:12–16. Why do you think God sent Elijah to the widow instead of someone who had plenty of food to spare?

_____

_____

_____

_____

Question 4

What does it look like to put God first in your life? Give some examples.

_____

_____

_____

_____

Question 5

Have there been times in your life when you've struggled to put God first? What was it like when you finally surrendered and gave Him your firstfruits?

_____

_____

_____

_____

PRAY

If studying alone, ask the Holy Spirit to reveal the truth about Himself to you. If in a group, take some time to pray for each other as you think about the truths discussed in this session.

EXPLORE

Do you want to go deeper with this teaching? Here are some additional things to think about, pray for, or write about in your journal throughout the next week.

Key Quote

I don't think God was giving us a list of rules. I think He was giving us a list of principles for living, and those principles enhance our relationship with Him and other people.

How does your opinion of the Ten Commandments change if you think about them as principles of relationship and not just a list of rules?

_____

_____

_____

_____

Key Verses
Exodus 20:3, 18-21; 1 Kings 17:12-16; Matthew 6:33; Romans 6:6
   What truths stand out to you as you read these verses?

_____

_____

   What is the Holy Spirit saying to you through these Scriptures?

_____

_____

Key Question
What is the Holy Spirit saying to you about putting God first in
your life?

Key Prayer
   Heavenly Father, we honor and praise You as the King of all kings
   and Lord of all lords. You are the only God, and we worship You
   and put You first in our lives. Show us any area of our lives that is
   not in order with Your commandments and help us to make You
   first in everything. In Jesus' name, Amen.

2

THE PRINCIPLE OF PURITY

When we keep God's second commandment to have no images or idols, our lives are free from bondage, and our generations are blessed.

RECAP

In the previous session, we learned that the Ten Commandments are more than a list of rules. God gave them to us as a set of principles by which we can establish better relationships with Him and others. The first principle is that we must put God first in everything.

In what ways did you put God first this past week?

ENGAGE

What fun things do you enjoy that are free of cost?

WATCH

Watch "The Principle of Purity."

- Look for the different things that constitute impurity before God and what causes them.
- Watch for the benefits and blessings of living a pure life.

(If you are not able to watch this teaching on video, read the following. Otherwise, skip to the **Talk** section after viewing.)

READ

The **principle of purity** is the principle behinds God's second commandment. Remember, the purpose of saying "You shall not" is to instruct, just as you would tell your child not to play in the street because you want to keep them safe.

> When you come into the land which the Lord your God is giving you, you shall not learn to follow the abominations of those nations. There shall not be found among you *anyone* who makes his son or his daughter pass through the fire, *or one* who practices witchcraft, *or* a soothsayer, or one who interprets omens, or a sorcerer, or one who conjures spells, or a medium, or a spiritist, or one who calls up the dead (Deuteronomy 18:9-11).

These were the kinds of practices that were taking place in the land the Israelites were entering. It was a nation of idolatry. God warned them not to make images like the pagans of Canaan did. In Acts 3:22 we read that Moses said God will raise up a Prophet from among them. He is saying that God has not appointed weird stuff for you like sorcerers and spiritists—God has appointed for you a personal relationship with Jesus Christ.

The Danger of Impurity

> You shall not make for yourself a carved image—any likeness *of anything* that *is* in heaven above, or that *is* in the earth beneath, or that *is* in the water under the earth (Exodus 20:4).

The Canaanites had more idols than any other nation. They made carved images as idols of their gods for almost everything. Israel was the only nation that did not worship images of their God. Note that Colossians 1:15 tells us, "He [Jesus] is the image of the invisible God."

The Canaanites had a national god as well as family gods and personal gods. They tricked the Israelites by telling them that they needed Asherah as their personal god and Baal as their family god. This is why all through the Old Testament, Israel built Asherah poles and Baal idols. God said the Canaanites would deceive them, and they did.

> So the children of Israel did evil in the sight of the Lord. They forgot the Lord their God, and served the Baals and Asherahs (Judges 3:7).

> Now therefore, send *and* gather all Israel to me on Mount Carmel, the four hundred and fifty prophets of Baal, and the four hundred prophets of Asherah, who eat at Jezebel's table (1 Kings 18:19).

At the same time God was telling Moses at the top of the mountain not to make carved images, the children of Israel were at the bottom of the mountain making two golden calves. And they said these calves—which they had just made—brought them out of Egypt!

The Canaanites believed that their gods lived in heaven and would put their spirits into the images they made. Then they used those idols to bless what they did. They used the fertility idol to help conceive. They paid for sex with temple prostitutes to "bless" their marriages. Then they sacrificed their children in fire to the false god Molech.

Any mixture of idols will bring impurity into your life. Satan gave the Canaanites the idea that the gods put their spirit into their images. Satan got that from God, who put an image of Himself on earth and put His spirit in it (Genesis 1:26).

Think about the word *image*. It is the root of the word *imagination*. If you imagine yourself with another spouse, or in another job, or with something else that God has not provided for you, you have an idol. Those are some of the dangers of impurity.

The Consequences of Impurity

> You shall not bow down to them, or serve them. For I, the Lord your God, *am* a jealous God, visiting the iniquity of the fathers upon the children to the third and fourth *generations* of those who hate Me (Exodus 20:5).

God *visits* the iniquities upon the children of those who hate God, not those who love Him. The grace of God is amazing. God visits these iniquities—he doesn't inhabit them. Most families in Israel had four generations living in one house. We have had four generations of our family in the house together. If my father showed up drunk at a gathering, it would affect all those present, including our children and grandchildren. God *visits* them because He is jealous for our affection.

God's jealousy is the good kind of jealousy. He is not angry at Israel; He is angry at those taking advantage of them. Therefore, He visits these generations so that they will see and consider the consequences of iniquity; they will seek God and break the curse.

The Jews even had a misinterpretation of that verse, saying that the son will die for the sins of their father. In Ezekiel God tells them no longer to say that, for He is a just God.

In Ezekiel 18:14, 17 God says that they can turn from those iniquities. My father grew up in an alcoholic family. But in our household, we never had a drop of alcohol, because he saw it, considered it, and turned away from it. He broke the generational curse.

The Blessings of Purity

In Exodus 20:6, God points out the blessings of purity to those who *love* Him:

But showing mercy to thousands, to those who love Me and keep My commandments.

Thousands here refers to generations. Deuteronomy 7:9 says, "Therefore know that the Lord your God, He *is* God, the faithful God who keeps covenant and mercy for a thousand generations with those who love Him and keep His commandments." So many times, we read the Old Testament and we see judgment . . . law . . . all this stuff. Yet all of it is for relationship. It's all for good. God doesn't

want you to walk in impurity because it affects your relationship
with Him. And it will affect your children and your grandchildren.

The word *showing* is also translated fashion, accomplish, prepare,
appoint, bring about, ordain, produce, press, or squeeze. God is
going to fashion mercy for you; accomplish mercy for you; prepare
mercy for you; appoint it; ordain it, bring it about, produce it, press
it, and squeeze blessings and mercy all over you and all over your
descendants. Simply love Him and keep His commandments. They
are not bad—they are good, and if we obey them, they will bless us
and our families.

NOTES

_____

_____

_____

_____

_____

_____

_____

_____

_____

TALK

These questions can be used for group discussion or personal reflection:

Question 1
Read Exodus 20:5 and Ezekiel 18:14, 17. Why does God allow iniquity to "visit" future generations?

_____

_____

_____

_____

Question 2
Read Genesis 1:26 and Colossians 1:15. Why does a pure relationship enable us to see Jesus as the image of the invisible God?

_____

_____

_____

_____

Question 3

Image is the root of imagination. What causes an imagination to form an idol? How does an idol cause weakness and an impure relationship with God?

_____

_____

_____

_____

Question 4

How does idol worship bring deadly consequences, as described in Psalm 106:36-38?

_____

_____

_____

Question 5

Read Exodus 20:5. What is the difference between the good jealousy that God has for us and selfish jealousy that is of the flesh?

_____

_____

_____

PRAY

If studying alone, ask the Holy Spirit to reveal the truth about Himself to you. If in a group, take some time to pray for each other as you think about the truths discussed in this session.

EXPLORE

Do you want to go deeper with this teaching? Here are some additional things to think about, pray for, or write about in your journal throughout the next week.

Key Quote

God doesn't want you to walk in impurity because it affects your relationship with Him. And it will affect your children and your grandchildren.

In what ways could God bless your children and grandchildren if you walk in purity?

_____

_____

_____

_____

Key Verses
Deuteronomy 18:9-11, 14-15; Exodus 20:4-6; Colossians 1:15;
Acts 3:22
What truths stand out to you as you read these verses?

_____

_____

What is the Holy Spirit saying to you through these Scriptures?

_____

_____

Key Question
In Judges 3:7 the Israelites forgot God and served the pagan gods
Asherah and Baal. Name some ways this happens in modern
society. How does keeping God's commands maintain purity in our
relationship with Him?

Key Prayer
Father, You have made us in Your image here on earth. Holy
Spirit, show us any image that is not of You that we have allowed
in our life. We repent and no longer serve it. We give it to You
and now receive Your deliverance. Thank You for sealing us into a
pure relationship with You. We praise You for generations to come
who will serve You only. In Jesus' name, Amen.

3

THE PRINCIPLE OF HUMILITY

God's name reveals His holy character. A humble Christian values and reveres the names of God in actions and in speech.

RECAP

In the previous session, we saw how important it is for us to remain pure in God's sight. We do this by abstaining from images and idols and worshipping only Him. When we do, He blesses current and future generations.

What things did you notice this week that could be idols or images (imaginations) in your life? How did you react to them?

ENGAGE

Did you have a nickname when you were a child? If so, what was it?

WATCH

Watch "The Principle of Humility."

- Look for the various names of God and how they reflect His character.
- Consider how you use the name of God in your everyday life.

(If you are not able to watch this teaching on video, read the following. Otherwise, skip to the **Talk** section after viewing.)

READ

You shall not take the name of the Lord your God in vain, for the Lord will not hold *him* guiltless who takes His name in vain (Exodus 20:7).

The third commandment demonstrates the **principle of humility**. It deals with how we relate to the names of God.

Why is God so insistent that we use His name in the right way? It is because His name describes who He is. When you hear that some person has a bad name in the community, you know that there is a character flaw in that person. A man's name refers to his character. It does not refer to the name on his birth certificate.

Even the Lord's prayer says, "Hallowed be thy name" (Matthew 6:9 KJV). *Hallowed* means "holy" or "separate." God's name is separate from every name on earth.

The name of God that is found over 6,800 times in the Old Testament is *Yahweh*. Yahweh and Jehovah are the same. The letters YHVH make up the name of God. There are no vowels in the Hebrew alphabet. It was in the thirteenth century that Catholics started to add vowels. The V came to be pronounced as W. *YaHWeH* means "He who caused existence." That's why God told Moses His name is "I Am That I Am" (Exodus 3:14 KJV)—*I was, I am, and I will be. I always existed.*

Israel went into exile around 590 BC because they profaned God's name. Jewish people stopped pronouncing God's name around 600 BC, in order to stop profaning His name. But the real way they were profaning His name was by *doing* the same things the pagans did. One of the greatest ways you profane the name of God is that you claim to be Christlike, yet you don't live like Christ.

In addition to not pronouncing God's name, many Jews even stopped writing it. We should be cautious, careful, and reverent when we use the name of God. Don't mix the holy with the profane.

> When they came to the nations, wherever they went, they profaned My holy name—when they said of them, "These *are* the people of the Lord, *and* yet they have gone out of His land." But I had concern for My holy name, which the house of Israel had profaned among the nations wherever they went.
>
> Therefore say to the house of Israel, "Thus says the Lord God: 'I do not do *this* for your sake, O house of Israel, but for My holy name's sake, which you have profaned among the nations wherever you went. And I will sanctify My great name, which has been profaned among the nations, which you have profaned in their midst; and the nations shall know that I *am* the Lord,' says the Lord God, 'when I am hallowed in you before their eyes'" (Ezekiel 36:20-23).

The word *take* means to "lift up" or "carry." God says we must not carry His name in a vain, empty, worthless. or prideful way. That is why I believe this commandment is about the principle of humility. I think that to call ourselves believers and be afraid that someone in the world is going to make fun of us or not accept us because we live a holy life is to use God's name in a vain way.

All through Scripture the name of the Lord is interchangeable with the Lord. Scriptures like Proverbs 18:10, Psalm 20:7, John 17: 6, 11–12, Romans 10:13, and Philippians 2:9 all talk about God's name. We know in all these verses that the name of the Lord is the same as the Lord.

This was extremely important to Jewish people because the Old Testament said "the God who is called by 'the name'." Every place in the New Testament where it says "the name" referring to Jesus, it says that you called on Yahweh, the name of God—and now Yahweh is here. God the Father has given Jesus "the name" that is above every name.

Prayer

The first way we can use the name of the Lord in a vain way is in prayer. The Israelites would call upon the names of their idols. But God meant that His name was not to be used as a magical incantation. Even in the New Testament this still happened:

> Then some of the itinerant Jewish exorcists took it upon themselves to call the name of the Lord Jesus over those who had evil spirits, saying, "We exorcise you by the Jesus whom Paul preaches." Also there were seven sons of Sceva, a Jewish chief priest, who did so.
>
> And the evil spirit answered and said, "Jesus I know, and Paul I know; but who are you?"

Then the man in whom the evil spirit was leaped on them, overpowered them, and prevailed against them, so that they fled out of that house naked and wounded. This became known both to all Jews and Greeks dwelling in Ephesus; and fear fell on them all, and the name of the Lord Jesus was magnified (Acts 19:13-17).

We use God's name in a vain or prideful way when we pray selfishly. James 4:3 says we don't receive when we pray wrongly. John 16:24 emphasizes the same principle. We pray correctly when we pray according to and for God's will.

Prophecy

Jeremiah 23:25 says, "I have heard what the prophets have said who prophesy lies in My name, saying, 'I have dreamed, I have dreamed!'" Ezekiel 22:28 says, "Her prophets plastered them with untempered *mortar*, seeing false visions, and divining lies for them, saying, 'Thus says the Lord God,' when the Lord had not spoken."

People in the Church today take the Lord's name in vain when they share their opinions and say that God said it. If you use the name of the Lord in vain, you will be punished.

Then I said, "Ah, Lord God! Behold, the prophets say to them, 'You shall not see the sword, nor shall you have famine, but I will give you assured peace in this place.'"

The Lord said to me, "The prophets prophesy lies in My name. I have not sent them, commanded them, nor spoken to them; they prophesy to you a false vision, divination, a worthless thing, and the deceit of their heart. Therefore thus says the Lord concerning the prophets who prophesy in My name, whom I did not send, and who say, 'Sword and famine shall not be in this land'—'By sword and famine those prophets shall be consumed!'" (Jeremiah 14:13-15).

The Lord said that the same thing the false prophets prophesied would come upon them. That is the result of false prophecy.

Proclamation

We can also speak the name of the Lord in the wrong way. Leviticus 19:12 says, "And you shall not swear by My name falsely, nor shall you profane the name of your God: I *am* the Lord." Leviticus 21:6 says, "They shall be holy to their God and not profane the name of their God." We have undervalued the name of God in our society. Even the saying "Oh, my God" contains no reverence. Yet we use OMG like LOL. And it is so arrogant that you would curse someone or something in God's name.

However, we can proclaim God's name in the right way:

In God we boast all day long,
and praise Your name forever (Psalm 44:8).

So I will sing praise to Your name forever,
That I may daily perform my vows (Psalm 61:8).

Sing out the honor of His name;
Make His name glorious (Psalm 66:2).

See also Psalm 100:4 and 113:3. The best way to proclaim the name of the Lord is with praise and gratitude.

It seems harsh that "the Lord will not hold him guiltless who takes His name in vain" (Exodus 20:7). But remember: Christ took our punishment. The commandments were given by grace. Here is a vital truth: God did not give the Ten Commandments to Israel while they were in Egypt. He didn't say, "You straighten up and act right, and then I'll deliver you from your enemies." God said, "I'll deliver you from your enemies and bury them in the Red Sea. And then after I save you by grace, I'll give you some principles to help you and me to have a better relationship."

That's the Ten Commandments. It was all by grace through faith. To walk through the Red Sea, the people of Israel had to believe that the walls would not come crashing in on them.

Jesus has taken your punishment. Keeping these principles will give you a deeper relationship with God and with other people.

NOTES

_____

_____

_____

_____

TALK

These questions can be used for group discussion or personal reflection:

Question 1

Many years before Christ was born, Israel went into exile because they profaned God's name by worshipping idols. Since God's name and His character are interchangeable, how does reverence for God's name influence how we live?

_____

_____

_____

_____

Question 2

In the Old Testament, the Jewish people said "the name" rather than pronouncing God's name. Read Romans 10:13 and John 1:12 in the New Testament. How has God honored that name of Jesus?

_____

_____

_____

_____

Question 3

Acts 19:13-16 tells us how the name of Jesus was improperly used. Read Acts 19:17. What caused the name of the Lord to be magnified?

Question 4

Read James 4:3 and John 16:24. How do the results of vain and selfish prayer compare with the results of praying for the will of God in His name?

Question 5

The first petition in the Lord's Prayer is "Hallowed be Thy name." How does this relate to the third commandment? In what ways does keeping this commandment make prayer effectual?

PRAY

If studying alone, ask the Holy Spirit to reveal the truth about Himself to you. If in a group, take some time to pray for each other as you think about the truths discussed in this session.

EXPLORE

Do you want to go deeper with this teaching? Here are some additional things to think about, pray for, or write about in your journal throughout the next week.

Key Quote

> God did not give the Ten Commandments to Israel while they were in Egypt. God didn't say, "You straighten up and act right, and then I'll deliver you from your enemies." God said, "I'll deliver you from your enemies and bury them in the Red Sea. And then after I save you by grace, I'll give you some principles to help you and me to have a better relationship."

In what way has God delivered you from your enemies?

_____

_____

_____

_____

Key Verses

Exodus 20:7; Ezekiel 36:20-23; Romans 10:13; John 1:12; 17:6, 11-12; Philippians 2:9

What truths stand out to you as you read these verses?

_____

_____

What is the Holy Spirit saying to you through these Scriptures?

_____

_____

Key Question

Read Philippians 2:9. What separates God's name from any other name? How does faith in His name set us apart as Christians?

Key Prayer

Father, forgive us for the times we have not revered Your name as we should. We receive Your forgiveness by faith, and we thank You, Jesus, for taking our punishment on the cross. We want to magnify Your holy name in our lives as we pray and listen to obey Your will. In Jesus' name, Amen.

4

THE PRINCIPLE OF REST

The Sabbath is God's gift to us. When we follow the commandment to rest, He restores and blesses us.

RECAP

In the previous session, we saw that the third commandment is a call for us to revere the name of the Lord and not take His name in vain. We must use God's name properly in prayer, prophecy, and proclamation.

Were you more aware this week of how the Lord's name was used by you and others? How did it make you feel when you heard His name used in a vain way?

ENGAGE

What is your favorite thing to do on weekends?

WATCH

Watch "The Principle of Rest."

- Look for the reasons that we rest.
- Consider how rest affects all areas of our lives.

(If you are not able to watch this teaching on video, read the following. Otherwise, skip to the **Talk** section after viewing.)

READ

The principle behind the fourth commandment is the **principle of rest**, and we find it in Exodus 20:8-11:

> Remember the Sabbath day, to keep it holy. Six days you shall labor and do all your work, but the seventh day *is* the Sabbath of the Lord your God. *In it* you shall do no work: you, nor your son, nor your daughter, nor your male servant, nor your female servant, nor your cattle, nor your stranger who *is* within your gates. For *in* six days the Lord made the heavens and the earth, the sea, and all that *is* in them, and rested the seventh day. Therefore the Lord blessed the Sabbath day and hallowed it.

Many believers today think we only have to obey nine of the Ten Commandments, with this fourth one being "optional." However, if we need to keep the other nine, why not this one too? I think we should, and there are good reasons to do so.

There Are Reasons God Said to Rest

Honoring the Sabbath gives God the opportunity to provide for us supernaturally.

> Then he said to them, "This *is what* the Lord has said: 'Tomorrow *is* a Sabbath rest, a holy Sabbath to the Lord. Bake what you will bake *today,* and boil what you will boil; and lay up for yourselves all that remains, to be kept until morning.'" So they laid it up till morning, as

Moses commanded; and it did not stink, nor were there any worms in it. Then Moses said, "Eat that today, for today *is* a Sabbath to the Lord; today you will not find it in the field. Six days you shall gather it, but on the seventh day, the Sabbath, there will be none."

Now it happened *that some* of the people went out on the seventh day to gather, but they found none. And the Lord said to Moses, "How long do you refuse to keep My commandments and My laws? See! For the Lord has given you the Sabbath; therefore He gives you on the sixth day bread for two days. Let every man remain in his place; let no man go out of his place on the seventh day." So the people rested on the seventh day (Exodus 16:23-30).

God gave the Israelites manna in the wilderness, but when they gathered more than they needed, the extra stank and got worms in it. On the Sabbath, though, they gathered what they needed for two days, and it did not stink. Still, some went out looking on the seventh day, and they found nothing. God had already told them, "You will not find it." Listen carefully: God will not provide for you if you work on the seventh day. The Lord gives us a *gift* on the Sabbath.

In Deuteronomy 5, God adds something to the story. He uses the word *observe*. He says the Israelites shouldn't work on the Sabbath because they had been slaves. When they were slaves in Egypt, they never got a day off. Only the wealthy and elite get a day off. We ourselves are often slaves to our work and our activities. God says He will take care of us. He says one day a week we are free, and He will provide for it. It is like tithing, in which God can do more with 90% than you can do with 100%. Similarly, God can do more in six days than you can in seven.

Sabbath gives us an opportunity to rest and be refreshed. Exodus 31:14–17 says,

> You shall keep the Sabbath, therefore, for *it is* holy to you. Everyone who profanes it shall surely be put to death; for whoever does *any* work on it, that person shall be cut off from among his people. Work shall be done for six days, but the seventh *is* the Sabbath of rest, holy to the Lord. Whoever does *any* work on the Sabbath day, he shall surely be put to death. Therefore the children of Israel shall keep the Sabbath, to observe the Sabbath throughout their generations *as* a perpetual covenant. It *is* a sign between Me and the children of Israel forever; for *in* six days the Lord made the heavens and the earth, and on the seventh day He rested and was refreshed.

This is a perpetual sign, and we have been grafted into this plan. Even back in Old Testament times, for thousands of years, keeping the Sabbath was a distinguishing sign that testified to other nations of God's creative power. It's a sign about what God did.

And though it says God rested and was refreshed, the word *refreshed* simply means to "take a breath." For six days God had been speaking and, thus, breathing out. On the seventh day, He breathed in. If God refreshes Himself, why don't you?

There Are Consequences When We Don't Rest

Now while the children of Israel were in the wilderness, they found a man gathering sticks on the Sabbath day. And those who found him gathering sticks brought him to Moses and Aaron, and to all the congregation. They put him under guard, because it had not been explained what should be done to him.

Then the Lord said to Moses, "The man must surely be put to death; all the congregation shall stone him with stones outside the camp." So, as the Lord commanded Moses, all the congregation brought him outside the camp and stoned him with stones, and he died (Numbers 15:32–36).

This is a pretty severe punishment. Not keeping the Sabbath was one of four things punishable by death at that time; murder, adultery, and rebellion against one's parents were the other three. Why would not keeping the Sabbath be up there with murder and adultery? Remember, there is a principle behind each commandment. Are you putting yourself to death by not resting one day a week? Are you killing yourself by refusing to honor the Sabbath?

In 2 Chronicles 36:20–21, we see that even the *land* had to fulfill its Sabbath. For 490 years the land had been plowed. God then kept His children out of the land for 70 years so that the land could be refreshed. If God is so concerned about the land, how much more is He concerned about you and me? Some of us are dying because we refuse to accept the gift of a day off.

There Are Blessings When We Rest

Mark 2:23–28 shows this principle of rest:

> Now it happened that He went through the grainfields on the Sabbath; and as they went His disciples began to pluck the heads of grain. And the Pharisees said to Him, "Look, why do they do what is not lawful on the Sabbath?"
>
> But He said to them, "Have you never read what David did when he was in need and hungry, he and those with him: how he went into the house of God *in the days* of Abiathar the high priest, and ate the showbread, which is not lawful to eat except for the priests, and also gave some to those who were with him?"
>
> And He said to them, "The Sabbath was made for man, and not man for the Sabbath. Therefore the Son of Man is also Lord of the Sabbath."

The Sabbath is not legalistic. The Sabbath is a gift to you. For me, since I work on Saturday, another day is my Sabbath. People ask me, *What do I do on Sabbath*? The real question is, *What do I not do?* I don't do anything related to work.

A number of years ago after an exceptionally long, exhausting schedule, I met with the elders and we created a policy where pastors get a sabbatical every five to seven years. It was my time, and I started an eight-week sabbatical. On day 53 of the sabbatical, I felt normal again. God revealed to me that I was feeling normal because I had fulfilled a full year of Sabbaths. I owed one year of

Sabbaths. God told me it wasn't because I owed Him those 52 days but because I owed myself those days. He told me never to go into debt again—with my time and my energy.

God gives you a day off. If you don't take it, then deep down you don't trust Him. It's the only reason you would work seven days a week when God commands to you take a rest.

NOTES

_____

_____

_____

_____

_____

_____

_____

_____

_____

_____

_____

_____

TALK

These questions can be used for group discussion or personal reflection:

Question 1

The definition of *Sabbath* is to "cease or stop labor." How would your schedule have to change if you were to do no work one day a week?

_____

_____

_____

_____

Question 2

What does God say about Sabbath rest in Exodus 20:8–11?

_____

_____

_____

_____

Question 3

What are some of the blessings we receive from honoring the Sabbath?

_____

_____

_____

_____

Question 4

How is honoring the Sabbath similar to tithing?

_____

_____

_____

_____

Question 5

Has God ever called you to an extended time of rest? If so, what happened?

_____

_____

_____

_____

PRAY

If studying alone, ask the Holy Spirit to reveal the truth about Himself to you. If in a group, take some time to pray for each other as you think about the truths discussed in this session.

EXPLORE

Do you want to go deeper with this teaching? Here are some additional things to think about, pray for, or write about in your journal throughout the next week.

Key Quote

Are you putting yourself to death by not resting one day a week? Are you killing yourself by refusing to honor the Sabbath?

What might the consequences be for not having a Sabbath rest? How serious could they be?

_____

_____

_____

_____

Key Verses
Exodus 20:8-11; 31:14-17; Numbers 15:32-36; Mark 2:23-28
What truths stand out to you as you read these verses?

_____

_____

What is the Holy Spirit saying to you through these Scriptures?

_____

_____

Key Question
How can we apply the concept of rest to our everyday lives?

Key Prayer
Lord, we thank You for the gift of Sabbath and the freedom to rest.
Help us use this holy day wisely. As we follow Your command,
bring refreshment, blessing, and spiritual insight to us. In Jesus'
name, Amen.

5

THE PRINCIPLE OF HONOR

God gave the command to honor your father and mother so that you would honor authority and have faith. When you believe in His promises, you can enjoy His blessings too.

RECAP

In the previous session, we learned about the principle of rest. Some people treat the fourth commandment as optional, but God gives us the Sabbath as a gift. If we will honor Him by giving Him one day, He will supernaturally bless us the other six days. What changes did you have to make to your schedule this past week in order to take a day off?

ENGAGE

What was your favorite family vacation? What made it so special?

WATCH

Watch "The Principle of Honor."

- Look for the things that honor produces in us at different stages of our lives.
- Watch for the results that accrue when we honor God.

(If you are not able to watch this teaching on video, read the following. Otherwise, skip to the **Talk** section after viewing.)

READ

W hy would God put honoring you parents on His top ten list? God is trying to instill the principle of honor in us when we are young because the consequences for dishonoring authority get more and more severe the older you get. It is foundational and imperative to understand the **principle of honor** if you want to have a happy and fulfilled life.

Honor Produces Faith

> Honor your father and your mother, that your days may be long upon the land which the Lord your God is giving you (Exodus 20:12).

God said that the people would live long in the *land* He was going to give them. Yet the majority of the Israelites who left Egypt did *not* enter the Promised Land. They were in the wilderness for 40 years, and everyone 20 years old or older died there. The only two exceptions were Joshua and Caleb. The others died before seeing God's Promised Land because they didn't honor the word of the Lord. Hebrews 3:19 says, "They could not enter in because of unbelief."

God wants us to learn to honor at an early age because if we won't honor our parents, we won't honor Him. Honor produces faith, but unbelief is a result of dishonor.

> Then He went out from there and came to His own country, and His disciples followed Him. And when the Sabbath had come, He began

to teach in the synagogue. And many hearing *Him* were astonished, saying, "Where *did* this Man *get* these things? And what wisdom *is* this which is given to Him, that such mighty works are performed by His hands! Is this not the carpenter, the Son of Mary, and brother of James, Joses, Judas, and Simon? And are not His sisters here with us?" So they were offended at Him.

But Jesus said to them, "A prophet is not without honor except in his own country, among his own relatives, and in his own house." Now He could do no mighty work there, except that He laid His hands on a few sick people and healed *them*. And He marveled because of their unbelief. (Mark 6:1-6).

"Familiarity breeds contempt" is a common phrase. *Familiarity* comes from the word "family." When we know people (family), we know all the bad things they've said and done, and we often don't give them their due honor. The people thought they knew all about Jesus, so they refused to honor Him.

Jesus marveled at the faith of the Roman centurion who told Jesus that He could heal his servant without Jesus having to come to his house. The centurion understood faith because he understood authority. The principle of honor is to honor those in authority. The reason that we may be the most faithless generation since the Book of Acts is because we are a very dishonoring generation.

God gave this commandment to honor your father and mother so that you would honor authority and have faith.

Honor Produces Blessings

Ephesians 6:1 says we should obey our parents and honor our mother and father. As a first step, we obey them when we are in their home as children. Then children grow up and move from obeying to honoring their parents. The promise is that things may go *well* with you and that you may live longer. Who wants to live longer if things aren't going well? Two siblings can come from the same parents and have different results; for one, things go well, and for the other, things don't go so well. The reason behind the difference is honor. Life goes well only for the person who respects and honors his parents.

Romans 13:1-2 tells us to be *subject* to governing authorities (a military term), and when we do, good things will happen. If not, there will be consequences. In Luke 2:51-52, we see that Jesus grew in wisdom and stature after he was *subject* to His parents. If Jesus was subject to His parents, we should also be subject to ours. We see the consequences of disobeying our parents in numerous Bible passages: Exodus 21:15, 17; Proverbs 20:20; Romans 1:30; and 2 Timothy 3:2.

Proverbs 30:11-17 describes a generation of entitlement that did not grow up honoring their parents. One of the first things Hitler did to change the nation of Germany was to encourage children to turn their parents in if they did not agree with Nazism. Today's generation suffers from the same lack of honor of authority.

Honor Produces Destiny

God has a Promised Land for you. He has a calling and a destiny on your life, and things will not go well with you if you don't honor your mother and father. God has a destiny—a Promised Land—for everyone. The Promised Land is not heaven. It is the overcoming Christian life on this earth.

In Matthew 15:1-8 Jesus rebukes the scribes and Pharisees as hypocrites for not honoring their parents with their traditions, even though they honored the commandment with their lips. Honor is not what you say; it's what you do, and it's what you do in your heart.

Some of you grew up with abusive or bad parents. You must still choose to honor them, based on this principle of honoring. Otherwise, bitterness and unforgiveness will destroy you. You can choose to live the principle of honor no matter what kind of parents you had. You can live a life of blessing in the land God is giving you.

NOTES

_____

_____

_____

_____

_____

_____

_____

TALK

These questions can be used for group discussion or personal reflection:

Question 1
Read Mark 6:1-6. How does honor affect belief?

_____

_____

_____

_____

Question 2
One of the definitions of *subject* is "to arrange in a military fashion under the command of a leader." According to Romans 13:1-2, what happens when we disregard this principle?

_____

_____

_____

_____

Question 3

What did Jesus do that enabled Him to increase in wisdom, stature, and favor in Luke 2:51-52? How can we follow His example?

_____

_____

_____

_____

Question 4

Read Proverbs 30:11-17. What are the characteristics of a dishonoring generation?

_____

_____

_____

_____

Question 5

Are there any authorities in your life whom you need to forgive? If yes, ask God to help you cultivate the principle of honor and break off any unforgiveness or bitterness.

_____

_____

_____

_____

PRAY

If studying alone, ask the Holy Spirit to reveal the truth about Himself to you. If in a group, take some time to pray for each other as you think about the truths discussed in this session.

EXPLORE

Do you want to go deeper with this teaching? Here are some additional things to think about, pray for, or write about in your journal throughout the next week.

Key Quote

> *Honor is not what you say; it's what you do, and it's what you do in your heart.*

Read Matthew 15:1-8. Why did Jesus call the scribes and Pharisees "hypocrites"?

_____

_____

_____

_____

Key Verses
Exodus 20:12; Mark 6:1-6; Proverbs 30:11-17; Romans 13:1-2
What truths stand out to you as you read these verses?

_____

_____

What is the Holy Spirit saying to you through these Scriptures?

_____

_____

Key Question
According to Ephesians 6:1-3, how does our attitude toward our parents change from childhood to adulthood?

Key Prayer
Father, I want to honor You with my words, actions, and heart. Please forgive me for the times I have dishonored the authorities in my life. Holy Spirit, please reveal any areas of bitterness or unforgiveness in my heart. I want to be a person of honor and faith. In Jesus' name, Amen.

6

THE PRINCIPLE OF LOVE

We must choose to give grace and forgiveness; otherwise, unresolved
anger will damage our lives.

RECAP

In the previous session, we learned that honoring our parents leads
to faith, blessings, and achieving our destiny. Dishonor, however,
produces unbelief and bitterness.

In what ways did you react differently to authority this week? Did
you find it easier to honor them?

ENGAGE

Besides Christmas, what is your favorite holiday and why?

WATCH

Watch "The Principle of Love."

- Look for the progression of offenses that end in hate and
  murder.
- Watch for the role of forgiveness in love.

(If you are not able to watch this teaching on video, read the
following. Otherwise, skip to the **Talk** section after viewing.)

READ

In Exodus 20:13, the sixth commandment says, "You shall not murder." Murder means taking a life when you don't have the authority to take that life. There are times when law enforcement, the military engaged in a war, or the judicial system takes a life. However, that is different from murder.

I call this commandment the **principle of love** because love is the opposite of murder, and because the Bible links murder to hate.

First John 3:15 says, "Whoever hates his brother is a murderer." In Romans 13:9 Paul sums up the last five commandments as, "You shall love your neighbor as yourself."

Murder itself is not a real concern of mine for those of you in our congregation. But I am concerned about the path that leads to murder.

Hate Precedes Murder

We see this in the story of Joseph. Genesis 37:4-5 says that Joseph's brothers hated him. In verse 18 they conspired to kill him. Deuteronomy 19:11-12 prescribed capital punishment for murder and linked hatred with murder. However, in Joshua 5 there was no punishment for killing someone accidentally, since there was no hate involved.

Anger Precedes Hate

The first murder in the Bible was because of anger (Genesis 4:3-5, 8). Cain was angry at Abel and killed him. Anger itself is an emotion, and you *can* be angry and not sin. It is what you do with anger that matters. Hate can develop when you don't deal with your anger. Unresolved anger can make you blow up and cause damage.

An Offense Precedes Anger

Cain was offended at God and at Abel. Matthew 24:10 says, "And then many will be offended, will betray one another, and will hate one another." The people were offended at Jesus in the story in Mark 6 where He was teaching in the temple (v. 3). As He began to teach, they got angry because He was just a carpenter. The same thing happened in Luke 4, when Jesus quoted from Isaiah and said that the prophecy of the Messiah was fulfilled that day. The people reacted the same way as they did in the Mark 6 story—they were filled with wrath and wanted to kill him (Luke 4:28-29). They were offended because He didn't meet their expectations.

Unfulfilled Expectations Precede Offenses

Then the disciples of John reported to him concerning all these things. And John, calling two of his disciples to *him,* sent *them* to Jesus, saying, "Are You the Coming One, or do we look for another?"

When the men had come to Him, they said, "John the Baptist has sent us to You, saying, 'Are You the Coming One, or do we look for another?'" And that very hour He cured many of infirmities, afflictions, and evil spirits; and to many blind He gave sight.

Jesus answered and said to them, "Go and tell John the things you have seen and heard: that *the* blind see, *the* lame walk, *the* lepers are cleansed, *the* deaf hear, *the* dead are raised, *the* poor have the gospel preached to them. And blessed is *he* who is not offended because of Me" (Luke 7:22–23).

In this remarkable passage, John the Baptist, Jesus' cousin, is in jail when Jesus arrives in the city. When Jesus does not come to see him, John sends his disciples to ask Jesus, "Are You the One?" Now remember, John was filled with the Spirit in his mother's womb. John once pointed at Jesus and said, "Behold the Lamb of God." John baptized Jesus and told others multiple times, "He's the One."

It appears John was bothered that Jesus had arrived and not visited or gotten him out of jail. So when Jesus responded, He implied that John shouldn't get offended because of Him. Unfulfilled expectations precede offenses. John thought Jesus would get him out of jail, or at least come to visit. When we have an expectation and it doesn't happen, we get offended.

Sometimes we get offended over silly or mundane things. The biblical definition of the word for *offense* is "stumbling stone." The Greek word is *scandalon*, from which we get the word scandal. Something becomes a stumbling stone to us. A *scandalon* is also the stick that you set up in front of a rabbit trap, which closes when the stick is moved. It is a snare. We actually give Satan the *scandalon* when we say something like, "If my husband ever did that, I'd never forgive him." Now Satan knows what snare to use.

Jesus is called "a stumbling stone and rock of offense" in Romans 9:33. Jesus is either going to be a stone you stumble over or a rock you build your house on.

When someone offends you and leaves a rock in your path, you can either stumble over it or step over it—or you can pick it up and carry it with you and show it to everybody else.

Forgiveness Precedes Love

Jesus tells us in Matthew 5:44 to love our enemies and do good to those who hate us. We do this through forgiveness. We see this summed up in the story of Jacob and Esau.

Genesis 27:4 says, "Esau hated Jacob because of the blessing with which his father blessed him, and Esau said in his heart, 'The days of mourning for my father are at hand; then I will kill my brother Jacob.'" Esau hated his brother, so he was going to kill him.

Twenty years later, in Genesis 33:1, we read, "Now Jacob lifted his eyes and looked, and there, Esau was coming, and with him were four hundred men." What would you think if the guy who had vowed to kill you was coming to greet you with 400 men? Here is verse 4: "But Esau ran to meet him, and embraced him, and fell on his neck and kissed him, and they wept."

How did Esau go from hating and wanting to murder his brother to embracing and kissing him? He forgave him.

Grace Precedes Forgiveness

Finally, grace precedes forgiveness. How do you forgive? Well, forgiveness is giving grace. So how do you give grace? You have to receive it. If you have a problem giving forgiveness, you have a problem receiving forgiveness. Jesus said, "Freely you have received, freely give" (Matthew 10:8). If you feel like you have to earn forgiveness from God, you'll make other people earn forgiveness from you. But once you understand grace, you will forgive.

Grace in the Greek means "release." When God forgave you, He released you from judgment. So when you truly forgive someone, you must truly release them. When people offend you, you forgive them.

NOTES

_____

_____

_____

_____

_____

_____

_____

_____

TALK

These questions can be used for group discussion or personal reflection:

Question 1

What is the difference between an individual committing murder and an authority, such as a judge, jury, or military rendering justice (Exodus 20:13)?

_____

_____

_____

_____

Question 2

Read Genesis 4:8. Have you ever been so angry that you have "blown up" over a situation? How can you avoid the consequences of unresolved anger?

_____

_____

_____

_____

Question 3

Read Mark 6:2-3 and Luke 4:28-29. Why were the people were so offended at Jesus?

_____

_____

_____

_____

Question 4

Read Luke 7:18-19, 22-23. Why do you think John the Baptist began to doubt who Jesus was?

_____

_____

_____

_____

Question 5

Why do some people have trouble giving forgiveness? What can they do about this problem?

_____

_____

_____

_____

PRAY

If studying alone, ask the Holy Spirit to reveal the truth about Himself to you. If in a group, take some time to pray for each other as you think about the truths discussed in this session.

EXPLORE

Do you want to go deeper with this teaching? Here are some additional things to think about, pray for, or write about in your journal throughout the next week.

Key Quote

> Forgiveness is giving grace. So how do you give grace? You have to receive it. If you have a problem giving forgiveness, you have a problem receiving forgiveness.

Do you have trouble receiving forgiveness? Begin thanking God for releasing you from the debt of sin and ask Him to show you how He sees you—as His precious, beloved child.

_____

_____

_____

_____

Key Verses

Luke 7:22-23; Genesis 4:3-5, 8; Matthew 24:10; Romans 9:33

What truths stand out to you as you read these verses?

_____

_____

What is the Holy Spirit saying to you through these Scriptures?

_____

_____

Key Question

Ask the Holy Spirit, "Am I withholding forgiveness from anyone? Whom do I need to release from judgment?"

Key Prayer

Father, thank You for sending Jesus to pay the price for my sins. I could never measure up to Your standards, but Your grace saved me. Please help me to show the same kindness to others. Today I choose to forgive those who have hurt, disappointed, and offended me, and I release them from my judgment. In Jesus' name, Amen.

7

THE PRINCIPLE OF INTIMACY

God is a Trinity, and we are also three parts. It is possible to commit adultery in body, soul, and spirit.

RECAP

In the previous session, we learned that murder is preceded by hate, which grows out of anger, offenses, and unfulfilled expectations. Love, on the other hand, comes from forgiveness and grace. We must learn to release others—and ourselves—from judgment.

What did you do when someone offended you this past week? Did you find it easy or difficult to release them from judgment?

ENGAGE

What is your earliest road trip memory? How would you compare the car and road conditions then to our present day?

WATCH

Watch "The Principle of Intimacy."
- Look for the three-part nature of God and man.
- Watch for how adultery affects all three parts of our being.

(If you are not able to watch this teaching on video, read the following. Otherwise, skip to the **Talk** section after viewing.)

READ

The principle behind the seventh commandment is the **principle of intimacy**. Exodus 20:14 says, "You shall not commit adultery." God gave us this principle to protect our intimacy with Him and with our spouse.

We are made of three parts—body, soul, and spirit—and adultery can be committed in each part.

Adultery in the Body

> Flee sexual immorality. Every sin that a man does is outside the body, but he who commits sexual immorality sins against his own body. Or do you not know that your body is the temple of the Holy Spirit *who is* in you, whom you have from God, and you are not your own? For you were bought at a price; therefore glorify God in your body and in your spirit, which are God's (1 Corinthians 6:18-20).

In today's society, many people get hung up on this commandment. They think it seems old-fashioned and outdated. But there is a principle and reasoning behind this commandment.

God created sex. He formed our sexual parts—male and female—to fit perfectly. God formed you to have pleasure and intimacy. It was His idea from the beginning.

There is a good sexual desire, and it is in marriage. The Greek word for *lust* is used by Jesus in Luke 22:15. It is just a strong desire. You don't have to be a prude to serve God. You can have fun in marriage.

Adultery in the Soul

Proverbs 6:32 says, "Whoever commits adultery with a woman lacks understanding; / He *who* does so destroys his own soul." Destroy means to corrupt, ruin, spoil, waste, and rot.

The soul is made up of the mind, will, and emotions. It is how you think about things, how you feel about things, and the decisions you make. You can commit adultery in your mind, and you can commit adultery in your emotions. You can have a wrong relationship in your mind with someone, and you can have a wrong relationship in your emotions with someone.

Any thought or feeling for another person that is inappropriate outside of marriage is wrong. Song of Solomon 3:5 says, "Do not stir up nor awaken love until it pleases." This means that it is pleasurable to God and to you in marriage. Just as there are things that lead to murder (such as anger and hate), adultery in the mind and emotions leads to bodily adultery.

Fantasy is *unrestrained* imagination. God designed you to live a fantasy with one person—your spouse. Marriage is designed to be fantastic.

In Matthew 5:27–28, Jesus says,

You have heard that it was said to those of old, "You shall not commit adultery." But I say to you that whoever looks at a woman to lust for her has already committed adultery with her in his heart.

The heart is made up of the soul and the spirit. This passage shows that lust precedes adultery and looking precedes lust. I have had to train myself not to look at other women. Potiphar's wife looked at Joseph with longing eyes. She looked before she lusted. David looked at Bathsheba from the balcony. Looking stirred up lust, which caused adultery.

Adultery in the Spirit

Something happens in the spirit that most of us don't realize is adultery.

> Therefore a man shall leave his father and mother and be joined to his wife, and they shall become one flesh (Genesis 2:24).

The husband and wife become one body in the flesh. They are joined together as one, and a man leaves his father and his mother and is joined (cleaves) to his wife. This Scripture is repeated four times in the New Testament. One of those times is in 1 Corinthians 6:15-20.

> Do you not know that your bodies are members of Christ? Shall I then take the members of Christ and make *them* members of a harlot? Certainly not! Or do you not know that he who is joined to a harlot is one body *with her?* For "the two," He says, "shall become one flesh." But he who is joined to the Lord is one spirit *with Him.*
> Flee sexual immorality. Every sin that a man does is outside the body, but he who commits sexual immorality sins against his own body. Or do you not know that your body is the temple of the Holy

Spirit *who is* in you, whom you have from God, and you are not your own? For you were bought at a price; therefore glorify God in your body and in your spirit, which are God's.

This same Scripture about marriage says that if a man, who is joined with his wife, then is joined to a harlot, he is also one body with her. There's a leaving and a cleaving. I've had parents tell me that they could tell when their teenager started having sex. I've had the offended party of a couple tell me they knew within a few weeks when their spouse began an affair. There's something that changed in the relationship.

In order to join yourself to someone else, you have to leave someone. So look at verse 17. When you are joined to the Lord, you become one spirit. When you commit adultery, you also leave something in the spirit. You lose your intimacy with God. You cannot have an intimate, committed, passionate relationship with Jesus if you are having an affair.

If there is a leaving, there is also a cleaving. And you have joined yourself to a demonic spirit. You open yourself up to not just one, but a family of them. When you commit adultery you have to lie, be deceptive, be manipulative, be prideful, be arrogant, be selfish and on and on. You have no idea how many spirits enter you when you leave the Lord and cleave to the dark world.

The good news is that God can redeem and restore. Do you know why God has so many "Thou shalt nots"? It's because

He wants you to be happy. He wants you to have a fulfilled, wonderful life.

Let me explain why any premarital or extramarital sex can destroy your life. In order to have premarital sex, you have to sneak around. You have to lie. You have to be deceptive. You develop a habit that God never intended for you to develop. You develop an appetite for sneaking around sex, and then you get married. You don't have to sneak around anymore, so that appetite cannot be satisfied. Thus, you find yourself sneaking around with someone else, and the cycle repeats.

So what do you do if you have had premarital sex or have committed adultery after marriage? Confess and repent. Bring it into the light. It may be very difficult at first, but I promise that confession is the first step to something wonderful the Lord has for your life.

NOTES

TALK

These questions can be used for group discussion or personal reflection:

Question 1

What does the word for "lust" in Luke 22:15 mean? What is the difference between good and bad lust?

_____

_____

_____

_____

Question 2

The New Testament tells us that Jesus grew up as a human while having a pure life. In what ways does this encourage and show us how to do the same?

_____

_____

_____

_____

Question 3

Read Proverbs 6:32. What does it mean for an adulterer to destroy his own soul?

_____

_____

_____

_____

Question 4

When a person commits adultery, what doors are open to demons?

_____

_____

_____

_____

Question 5

Job 31:1 says, "I have made a covenant with my eyes." How can we make the same covenant? Why does it make purity easier to maintain?

_____

_____

_____

_____

PRAY

If studying alone, ask the Holy Spirit to reveal the truth about Himself to you. If in a group, take some time to pray for each other as you think about the truths discussed in this session.

EXPLORE

Do you want to go deeper with this teaching? Here are some additional things to think about, pray for, or write about in your journal throughout the next week.

Key Quote

Do you know why God has so many "Thou shalt nots"? It's because He wants you to be happy. He wants you have a fulfilled, wonderful life.

In what ways do you see God's commandments bringing happiness and fulfillment in your life?

_____

_____

_____

_____

Key Verses
1 Corinthians 6:15-20; Proverbs 6:32; Genesis 2:24;
Matthew 5:27-28

What truths stand out to you as you read these verses?

_____

_____

What is the Holy Spirit saying to you through these Scriptures?

_____

_____

Key Question
Why is sexual immorality a sin against one's own body? How does
this affect your oneness with Christ?

Key Prayer
Lord, You are faithful in all Your ways. We want to be faithful to
You in body, soul, and spirit. Lead us into greater intimacy with
the Holy Spirit. We cleave to You and walk on Your path. Your
perfect love has redeemed us and keeps us until the glorious day
when we finally see You face to face. In Jesus' name, Amen.

8

THE PRINCIPLE OF TRUST

When you trust God, you won't steal, because you trust Him to provide for you.

RECAP

In the previous session, we learned that we can commit adultery in our body, soul, and spirit. God gave us the principle of intimacy because He wants us to enjoy our relationship with Him and have a fantastic marriage.

Did you have any opportunity this week to control improper thoughts or feelings?

ENGAGE

What is your favorite book or television show?

WATCH

Watch "The Principle of Trust."

- Look for the ways we steal from God as well as from others.
- Consider your heart and your approach to giving.

(If you are not able to watch this teaching on video, read the following. Otherwise, skip to the **Talk** section after viewing.)

READ

The eighth commandment is "You shall not steal" (Exodus 20:15). The principle behind this commandment is the **principle of trust**. There is really only one reason why anyone would steal: you don't trust God to provide for you.

Ephesians 4 refers to several of the commandments. Verse 28 says, "Let him who stole steal no longer, but rather let him labor, working with *his* hands what is good, that he may have something to give him who has need."

Stop Stealing

If you're going to develop this concept of trust in your life, you're going to have to stop stealing in little ways. I think we sometimes steal and excuse our behavior because what we stole was "only a little thing."

This is the thing which the Lord has commanded: "Let every man gather it according to each one's need, one omer for each person, *according to the* number of persons; let every man take for *those* who *are* in his tent."

Then the children of Israel did so and gathered, some more, some less. So when they measured *it* by omers, he who gathered much had nothing left over, and he who gathered little had no lack. Every man had gathered according to each one's need (Exodus 16:16–18).

Notice that God provides each day the exact amount every person needs. Therefore, if you took more than you were supposed to take, you would be stealing from another person.

Remember there is a tremendous difference between *taking more* and *making more*. The problem in America today is not those who are making more; the problem is those who are taking more. Those who are making more create jobs and grow the economy. Those who feel they are entitled and take more are bad for the economy. That's stealing.

God provided enough on the sixth day for two days, but some people went out to gather on the seventh day. God responded to this in Exodus 16:28: "And the Lord said to Moses, 'How long do you refuse to keep My commandments and My laws?'" Keep means a guard or a *trustworthy* keeper. God is saying, *How long do you refuse to trust Me*? Israel didn't trust that God would provide enough on the sixth day for two days. Stealing is a bold statement to God that you don't trust Him to provide.

Christians still steal today. Have you bought anything on an expense account that really was personal? Have you ever charged something to the company that was personal? God expects us to have integrity in everything we charge. Taking a longer lunch than allowed or asking to be paid in cash so as not to pay tax on it is stealing. Not paying one's debts or not working the agreed number of hours is stealing. Since the Lord owns everything (Psalm 24:1), when you steal from anyone, you are stealing from the Lord. Satan is the master thief (see John 10:10). If you steal, you work in darkness and deceit like Satan.

Start Working

Part two of Ephesians 4:28 says to labor. Many people have jobs but don't really work. Labor means to grow weary, tired, and to be *exhausted*. Work means to earn something. God blesses hard work. The fourth commandment balances the eighth—you need rest when you work. God put Adam and Eve in the garden to work (Genesis 2:15). Work is supposed to be a joy: "For my heart rejoiced in all my labor; / And this was my reward from all my labor (Ecclesiastes 2:10). The reward was the work. Work brings rewards and joy. If you want to trust God for provision, stop stealing and start working.

Get Giving

The last part of Ephesians 4:28 says to work so that "he *may* have something to give him who has need." Note the word *may*. We don't have to give—we get to give. God's not going to make you give. Let me say it another way: We get to give; we don't give to get. If we don't steal, and if we work hard, we can contribute to those who have a real need.

Probably the biggest theft going on in the church is taking what belongs to God. Joshua 6:19 says, "But all the silver and gold, and vessels of bronze and iron, *are* consecrated to the Lord; they shall come into the treasury of the Lord." This was the tithe. In 7:11 we read

"Israel has sinned, and they have also transgressed My covenant which I commanded them. For they have even taken some of the accursed things, and have both stolen and deceived; and they have also put *it* among their own stuff."

Just as you have to be deceptive when you commit adultery, you have to be deceptive when you steal. You have to learn deceit.

The root of the word *stealthy* is steal. The thief learns to be deceptive, in darkness, so as not to get caught. Achan took these things as Israel was getting ready to enter the Promised Land, a land flowing with milk and honey. Yet he never gets to enter it because of his stealing. This was the tithe for God's storehouse. How ironic.

God wants you to trust Him. We see this all through the Bible. Adam and Eve didn't trust God enough to keep from eating from the tree of the knowledge of good and evil. Cain didn't trust God enough to give the firstfruits. God asked for all the silver and gold from Jericho because it was the first.

If you try to provide for yourself, you'll have to do that for the rest of your life. It's so much better living in the provision of God. It's all through Scripture. Trust God even though there's a lion's den; a fiery furnace; an Egyptian army behind you and the Red Sea in front of you. Stretch out your hand. Get out of the boat. Rise and walk. God's saying, "Trust Me."

Most eastern cultures invoke the death penalty for stealing, but Israel did not. God came up with the plan of restitution. Restitution is composed of two words—one meaning to restore and the other meaning to remove guilt and shame. God gives you the chance to give back what you've stolen so that you don't have to continue living in guilt and shame. When we repent, God forgives us and allows us to make things right. God's already forgiven us through Christ, but He also wants to remove the guilt and shame.

NOTES

_____

_____

_____

_____

_____

_____

_____

_____

_____

_____

_____

_____

TALK

These questions can be used for group discussion or personal reflection:

Question 1

Read John 10:10. Why does Satan want to steal from believers?

_____

_____

_____

_____

Question 2

In what ways does Joshua 6:19 refer to the firstfruits of labor? Why would lack of trust prevent God's blessing?

_____

_____

_____

_____

Question 3

List some common ways of stealing our culture might find accept-able. How can an entitlement mentality deceive a person to steal rather than trust God?

_____

_____

_____

_____

Question 4

What is the difference between *making* more than you need and *taking* more than you need?

_____

_____

_____

_____

Question 5

Read Exodus 16:25–28. How does resting from hard work on the Sabbath show trust in God's provision?

_____

_____

_____

_____

PRAY

If studying alone, ask the Holy Spirit to reveal the truth about Himself to you. If in a group, take some time to pray for each other as you think about the truths discussed in this session.

EXPLORE

Do you want to go deeper with this teaching? Here are some additional things to think about, pray for, or write about in your journal throughout the next week.

Key Quote

Work brings rewards and joy. If you want to trust God for provision, stop stealing and start working.

How does hard work bring joy to your life?

_____

_____

_____

_____

Key Verses

Exodus 20:15; Ephesians 4:28; Exodus 16:16–18, 28; Joshua 6:19; 7:11

What truths stand out to you as you read these verses?

_____

_____

What is the Holy Spirit saying to you through these Scriptures?

_____

_____

Key Question

Are there any areas of your life in which you struggle to trust God for provision?

Key Prayer

Father, thank You for Your provision for us. Please show us where we have stolen from You or others, so we can repent and turn to You. Help us guard our ways to trust You for provision, rest, and restoration. In Jesus' name, Amen.

9

THE PRINCIPLE OF HONESTY

When we are honest and transparent, we are free to have better
relationships with God and everyone else with whom we interact.

RECAP

In the previous session, we learned that stealing shows a lack of trust in God. When we trust God for provision, He will provide for us. We show trust by working hard and giving our firstfruits to Him. Did you find it easier to trust in God for your provision this past week?

ENGAGE

If you could take an extra day or two off work, what would you do for fun?

WATCH

Watch "The Principle of Honesty."

- Look for the different ways that we demonstrate honesty.
- Consider how God wants us to deal with dishonesty.

(If you are not able to watch this teaching on video, read the following. Otherwise, skip to the **Talk** section after viewing.)

READ

You shall not bear false witness against your neighbor (Exodus 20:16).

The ninth commandment brings the **principle of honesty**. Yes, this commandment means you shouldn't lie, but there is so much more to it. Also, your "neighbor" is more than just someone you live near; it includes anyone in your life. Jesus made that clear when He told the story of the good Samaritan.

God was establishing a society, and the Ten Commandments were its foundation. A civilized society is one governed by moral laws. Morality is not subjective—it is objective, based on the truth of the Bible. This commandment was a legal mandate against perjury.

Disputes were settled in those days by a court of the elders (men over age 50) of a tribe or a clan. The main way of deciding guilt or innocence at that time was by witnesses. Some people hired false witnesses, but if you were found to give false testimony in a capital/murder case, you were also guilty of murder. And according to the law, if a person was to be stoned to death, the witnesses had to cast the first stone. Other ancient cultures also had stiff perjury laws. The American oath to "tell the truth, the whole truth, and nothing but the truth, so help me God" comes from this as well.

Most of you won't perjure yourself in a murder trial, but we need to honor the principle of honesty. There are many ways to lie. We need to call sin what it is: *sin!*

Here are three simple ways to develop honesty in your life.

Be Honest with Yourself

The hardest people to help are those who won't be honest with themselves. Some carry very deep and painful wounds from their past. They have yet to experience God's healing, so they use excuses to avoid facing the truth. However, God won't help you if you won't be honest with yourself. Humans make mistakes all the time, and if you can't be honest about your mistakes, you'll never be free.

I tend to exaggerate, and I have asked for accountability for that. Exaggeration isn't just a "mistake"; it's a lie. But people will forgive you when you catch yourself and say, "That's not right." Honest people admit their mistakes and accept correction.

Be Honest with Others

Sometimes people say, "I'm going to be honest with you now." Yes, it's just an expression, but it also implies that they weren't being honest before.

God takes honesty with others seriously. James 5:16 says, "Confess *your* trespasses to one another, and pray for one another, that you may be healed." You may wonder, *Why can't I just confess to God?* When we confess to others as well as God, we gain humility and accountability. You need to talk with someone about your sin in order to bring it out of the darkness and into the light.

The Bible talks about three types of people: wise, foolish, and evil. A wise person can be corrected, and he'll be wiser still. He'll adapt himself to the truth. A foolish person, however, will make excuses. Instead of receiving the truth, he will adapt it to himself (see Proverbs 9:8). You cannot correct fools with words; they respond only to consequences. Evil people never receive the truth, and Titus 3:10 says to reject them after two warnings.

Honesty brings freedom. Many people have two personalities — one public and one private. When you are honest, though, you don't have to be two people anymore.

Be Honest with God

Can you imagine how God feels when you are dishonest with Him? Do you think He doesn't know that thing you did last week? Do you think you're smarter than Him?

Here's the amazing thing: God not only knows about what you did, but He also knew you'd do it, and He's already paid for it—in full! You may think you can deal with it yourself without confessing to God, but that is pride. It should be just the opposite. You need to bring God into it and tell Him everything.

After his affair with Bathsheba, David wrote:

Blessed *is he whose* transgression *is* forgiven,
Whose sin *is* covered.
Blessed *is* the man to whom the Lord does not impute iniquity,
And in whose spirit *there is* no deceit.
When I kept silent, my bones grew old
Through my groaning all the day long.
For day and night Your hand was heavy upon me;
My vitality was turned into the drought of summer. *Selah*

I acknowledged my sin to You,

And my iniquity I have not hidden.

I said, "I will confess my transgressions to the Lord,"

And You forgave the iniquity of my sin (Psalm 32:1-5).

Here is what David is saying: *Until I confessed my sin, I felt horrible. I had no vitality, no strength, no peace.* What took him so long to confess? Look at verse 2: "Blessed *is* the man to whom the Lord does not impute iniquity, / And in whose spirit *there is* no deceit." When you are dishonest, you are deceived in your spirit. You need to be transparent and fully vulnerable with God and with others.

I had to deal with this issue at one time. It was seven years into my marriage, and I was going through a restoration process. I wrote down everything I remembered that I had done wrong and shared it with my pastor, Olen Griffing, and with Debbie.

When I finished telling Debbie (it took several hours), she said to me, "Robert, I knew you were bad when I married you. I didn't know you were *that* bad, but I knew you were bad. But I loved you, and I saw in you a person who wanted to deal with the sin he was involved in. I loved you then, but I love you more today because you've been honest with me."

I've counseled many couples, and the hardest thing for those who have experienced infidelity in their marriage is not the immorality; it's the dishonesty.

God wants you to be honest. He wants you to be honest with yourself, with others, and with Him. Start being an honest person today.

NOTES

_____

_____

_____

_____

_____

_____

_____

_____

_____

_____

_____

_____

_____

_____

TALK

These questions can be used for group discussion or personal reflection:

Question 1

How is the principle of honesty more than just not telling lies?

_____

_____

_____

_____

Question 2

Why do you think dishonest people are the hardest people to help?

_____

_____

_____

_____

Question 3

Read James 5:16. Why do we need to be honest with others as well as God?

_____

_____

_____

_____

Question 4
How does a wise person deal with correction differently than a foolish person?

_____

_____

_____

_____

Question 5
Read Psalm 32:1–5. How did David feel before he confessed his sin to God? How did he feel afterward?

_____

_____

_____

_____

PRAY

If studying alone, ask the Holy Spirit to reveal the truth about Himself to you. If in a group, take some time to pray for each other as you think about the truths discussed in this session.

EXPLORE

Do you want to go deeper with this teaching? Here are some additional things to think about, pray for, or write about in your journal throughout the next week.

Key Quote

> *Many people have two personalities—one public and one private. When you are honest, though, you don't have to be two people anymore.*

Who are some friends or family members with whom you can start being totally honest?

_____

_____

_____

_____

Key Verses
Exodus 20:16; James 5:16; Psalm 32:1-5
What truths stand out to you as you read these verses?

_____

_____

What is the Holy Spirit saying to you through these Scriptures?

_____

_____

Key Question
Why is honesty so important to the success of a civilized society?
How has the lack of honesty affected today's world?

Key Prayer
Father, we want to be people of integrity who walk in Your light.
Help us to be honest with ourselves, others, and You. Holy Spirit,
show us any areas of deception in our hearts and please forgive us
for not being honest. Thank You for cleansing us and making us
holy like You. In Jesus' name, Amen.

10

THE PRINCIPLE OF CONTENTMENT

Satan can make something look good that does not belong to you, so you develop a strong desire that is not from God. God's commandment not to covet strengthens our relationship with Him through trust and contentment.

RECAP

In the previous session, we discovered that being honest improves our relationship with God and other people. We must learn to be open and transparent with ourselves, others, and God.

Did you find it easier to be honest with yourself this past week? What about with others and with God?

ENGAGE

What is your least favorite household chore?

WATCH

Watch "The Principle of Contentment."

- Look for the definition of coveting and how it relates to lust.
- Watch for the ways you are able to develop contentment.

(If you are not able to watch this teaching on video, read the following. Otherwise, skip to the **Talk** section after viewing.)

READ

You shall not covet your neighbor's house; you shall not covet
your neighbor's wife, nor his male servant, nor his female servant,
nor his ox, nor his donkey, nor anything that *is* your neighbor's
(Exodus 20:17).

The tenth principle is the **principle of contentment**. The only
reason we would covet what someone else has is if we are not
content with what we have.

Hebrews 13:5 shows how contentment is the opposite, or the
remedy, to covetousness.

Let your conduct *be* without covetousness; *be* content with such
things as you have. For He Himself has said, "I will never leave you
nor forsake you."

That is a quote from Joshua 1:5 after Moses died. God said He
would be with Joshua just as He was with Moses. He told the new
leader, *The way you can be content is that I will never leave you nor
forsake you. I'll always be your Father. I'll always be your Provider.*

What Is Coveting?

The Ten Commandments are also in Deuteronomy 5, and there
they are a little different.

You shall not covet your neighbor's wife; and you shall not desire your neighbor's house, his field, his male servant, his female servant, his ox, his donkey, or anything that *is* your neighbor's (Deuteronomy 5:21).

We like to boil this commandment down to "Do not covet," which is okay, so long as we understand what covet means. The word *covet* means "to strongly desire." The whole commandment does not mean that you shall not have desires. God believes in owning personal property. What He is saying is that you should not desire what belongs to someone else. We should not want what our neighbor has.

Like many things in the Bible, this goes back to Genesis. Satan got Adam and Eve to covet the one tree God owned and forbade them to eat from:

So when the woman saw that the tree *was* good for food, that it *was* pleasant to the eyes, and a tree desirable to make *one* wise, she took of its fruit and ate. She also gave to her husband with her, and he ate (Genesis 3:6).

Satan will do everything he can to make what your neighbor has look better (more desirable) than what you have. (Remember that your neighbor is anyone you encounter.) Covetousness then causes us to resent God. We begin to think, *If God is providing for him, why not for me?*

Covetousness is serious.

> He said to them, "Take heed and beware of covetousness, for one's
> life does not consist in the abundance of the things he possesses"
> (Luke 12:15).

If you've been blessed financially—and compared to the rest of the
world, most of us in America have been—that would be a good
Scripture to memorize. Jesus says beware of covetousness. In his
letter to the people of Corinth, Paul lists covetousness with other
serious sins, such as sexual immorality, idolatry, and extortion (see
1 Corinthians 5:11–12).

Ephesians 5:3 says that fornication and all uncleanness or covetousness should not be found among the saints. And Colossians 3:5
explains why covetousness is so bad:

> Therefore put to death your members which are on the earth:
> fornication, uncleanness, passion, evil desire, and covetousness,
> which is idolatry.

Why is covetousness idolatry? Because you are putting someone,
or something, above God. That thing or person has now become an
idol in your life. If you begin to covet something, you will actually
exchange God for it. Without realizing it, people think, *I'll give everything I have for that person's wife, that job, or that neighborhood.*

God is incredibly clear in this commandment: don't covet *anything* that is your neighbor's. It's alright to have a desire, but God says it is wrong to have a strong desire for something that belongs to someone else.

Contentment vs. Contention

The root of these words is the same. *Content* means "happy" or "satisfied." The suffix *ment* means "the state of." The suffix *ion* means there is a "struggle" or a "quarrel." *Contention* means "competition." If you are not content, you are not in a state of contentment; you are in a state of contention. Competition is a sister word to comparison. When we are not content, we compare. We compare our house, our job, or our spouse to someone else's. Comparison shows dissatisfaction compared to what someone else has. This can only result in either a feeling of inferiority or superiority.

Coveting won't allow you to rejoice when someone else gets blessed. If something good happens to someone you don't like, you get mad. Or if something bad happens to someone you don't like, you might rejoice a little bit. Comparison is never right: "For we dare not class ourselves or compare ourselves with those who commend themselves. But they, measuring themselves by themselves, and comparing themselves among themselves, are not wise" (2 Corinthians 10:12). One reason people are foolish is that they are always comparing themselves. And this society is worse than any other because of social media. Social media is not real. We only see what someone wants us to see—and then we covet it.

Delight Before Desires

Delight yourself also in the Lord,
And He shall give you the desires of your heart (Psalm 37:4).

This Scripture is often misapplied. Most people think this verse means if you serve the Lord, He'll give you what you want. That's not what it means, though. What David is actually saying is if you delight yourself in the Lord—if you trust and serve Him—He will put the right desires in your heart. Once you come to the place where you're content with what God's provided for you, you won't be comparing yourself with other people, and you will never have to worry about coveting.

NOTES

_____

_____

_____

_____

_____

_____

_____

_____

_____

TALK

These questions can be used for group discussion or personal reflection:

Question 1

What is the definition of the word *covet*? Why do people struggle with covetousness?

_____

_____

_____

_____

Question 2

Read 1 Corinthians 5:11–12. Why do you think Paul lists covetousness with serious sins, such as sexual immorality and extortion?

_____

_____

_____

_____

Question 3
What is the difference between contentment and comparison?

_____

_____

_____

_____

Question 4
What role does social media play when it comes to covetousness?

_____

_____

_____

_____

Question 5
Read Psalm 37:4. How do most people misinterpret this verse?
What is the real meaning?

_____

_____

_____

_____

PRAY

If studying alone, ask the Holy Spirit to reveal the truth about Himself to you. If in a group, take some time to pray for each other as you think about the truths discussed in this session.

EXPLORE

Do you want to go deeper with this teaching? Here are some additional things to think about, pray for, or write about in your journal throughout the next week.

Key Quote

If you delight yourself in the Lord—if you trust and serve Him—He will put the right desires in your heart.

What are some desires that are in your heart today? Are they the result of comparison or are they based on your delight in the Lord?

_____

_____

_____

_____

Key Verses

Exodus 20:17; Deuteronomy 5:21; Genesis 3:6; 1 Corinthians 5:11;
Ephesians 5:3; Philippians 4:11; Psalm 37:4

What truths stand out to you as you read these verses?

_____

_____

What is the Holy Spirit saying to you through these Scriptures?

_____

_____

Key Question

How does coveting lead to idolatry and resentment?

Key Prayer

Father, Your Word promises us that You will never leave us.
Thank You for making us joint heirs in the body of Christ. Holy
Spirit, please convict us of any areas of our lives in which we are
not trusting You for provision. You promised to give us everything
we need, and we choose to trust You. In Jesus' name, Amen.

LEADER'S GUIDE

The *RELATIONSHIP* Leader's Guide is designed to help you lead your small group or class through the *RELATIONSHIP* curriculum. Use this guide along with the curriculum for a life-changing, interactive experience.

BEFORE YOU MEET

- Ask God to prepare the hearts and minds of the people in your group. Ask Him to show you how to encourage each person to integrate the principles all of you discover into your daily lives through group discussion and writing in your journals.
- Preview the video segment for the week.
- Plan how much time you'll give to each portion of your meeting (see the suggested schedule below). In case you're unable to get through all of the activities in the time you have planned, here is a list of the most important questions (from the **Talk** section) for each week.

SUGGESTED SCHEDULE FOR THE GROUP:

1. **Engage** and **Recap** (5 Minutes)
2. **Watch** or **Read** (20 Minutes)
3. **Talk** (25 Minutes)
4. **Pray** (10 minutes)

SESSION ONE

Q: How does tithing demonstrate that God is first in our lives?

Q: Read 1 Kings 17:12–16. Why do you think God sent Elijah to the widow instead of someone who had plenty of food to spare?

SESSION TWO

Q: Image is the root of imagination. What causes an imagination to form an idol? How does an idol cause weakness and an impure relationship with God?

Q: Read Exodus 20:5. What is the difference between the good jealousy that God has for us and selfish jealousy that is of the flesh?

SESSION THREE

Q: Many years before Christ was born, Israel went into exile because they profaned God's name by worshipping idols. Since God's name and His character are interchangeable, how does reverence for God's name influence how we live?

Q: Read James 4:3 and John 16:24. How do the results of vain and selfish prayer compare with the results of praying for the will of God in His name?

SESSION FOUR

Q: The definition of *Sabbath* is to "cease or stop labor." How would your schedule have to change if you were to do no work one day a week?

Q: How is honoring the Sabbath similar to tithing?

SESSION FIVE

Q: Read Mark 6:1-6. How does honor affect belief?

Q: What did Jesus do that enabled Him to increase in wisdom, stature, and favor in Luke 2:51-52? How can we follow His example?

SESSION SIX

Q: Read Genesis 4:8. Have you ever been so angry that you have "blown up" over a situation? How can you avoid the consequences of unresolved anger?

Q: Read Mark 6:2-3 and Luke 4:28-29. Why were the people were so offended at Jesus?

SESSION SEVEN

Q: What does the word for "lust" in Luke 22:15 mean? What is the difference between good and bad lust?

Q: When a person commits adultery, what doors are open to demons?

SESSION EIGHT

Q: List some common ways of stealing our culture might find acceptable. How can an entitlement mentality deceive a person to steal rather than trust God?

Q: Read Exodus 16:25-28. How does resting from hard work on the Sabbath show trust in God's provision?

SESSION NINE

Q: Read James 5:16. Why do we need to be honest with others as well as God?

Q: How does a wise person deal with correction differently than a foolish person?

SESSION TEN

Q: What is the definition of the word *covet*? Why do people struggle with covetousness?

Q: Read Psalm 37:4. How do most people misinterpret this verse? What is the real meaning?

HOW TO USE THE CURRICULUM

This study has a simple design.

EACH WEEK

The One Thing

This is a brief statement under each session title that sums up the main point—the key idea—of the session.

Recap

Recap the previous week's session, inviting members to share about any opportunities they have encountered throughout the week that apply what they learned (this doesn't apply to the first week).

Engage

Ask the icebreaker question to help get people talking and feeling comfortable with one another.

Watch
Watch the videos (recommended).

Read
If you're unable to watch the videos, read these sections.

Talk
The questions in these lessons are intentionally open-ended. Use them to help the group members reflect on Scripture and the lesson.

Pray
Ask members to share their concerns and then pray together. Be sensitive to the Holy Spirit and the needs of the group.

Explore
Encourage members to complete the written portion in their books before the next meeting.

KEY TIPS FOR THE LEADER

- Generate participation and discussion.
- Resist the urge to teach. The goal is for great conversation that leads to discovery.
- Ask open-ended questions—questions that can't be answered with "yes" or "no" (e.g., "What do you think about that?" rather than "Do you agree?")

- When a question arises, ask the group for their input instead of answering it yourself before allowing anyone else to respond.
- Be comfortable with silence. If you ask a question and no one responds, rephrase the question and wait for a response. Your primary role is to create an environment where people feel comfortable to be themselves and participate, not to provide the answers to all of their questions.
- Ask the group to pray for each other from week to week, especially about key issues that arise during your group time. This is how you begin to build authentic community and encourage spiritual growth within the group.

KEYS TO A DYNAMIC SMALL GROUP

Relationships

Meaningful, encouraging relationships are the foundation of a dynamic small group. Teaching, discussion, worship, and prayer are important elements of a group meeting, but the depth of each element is often dependent upon the depth of the relationships between members.

Availability

Building a sense of community within your group requires members to prioritize their relationships with one another. This means being available to listen, care for one another, and meet each other's needs.

Mutual Respect

Mutual respect is shown when members value each other's opinions (even when they disagree) and are careful never to put down or embarrass others in the group (including their spouses, who may or may not be present).

Openness

A healthy small group environment encourages sincerity and transparency. Members treat each other with grace in areas of weakness, allowing each other room to grow.

Confidentiality

To develop authenticity and a sense of safety within the group, each member must be able to trust that things discussed within the group will not be shared outside the group.

Shared Responsibility

Group members will share the responsibility of group meetings by using their God-given abilities to serve at each gathering. Some may greet, some may host, some may teach, etc. Ideally, each person should be available to care for others as needed.

Sensitivity

Dynamic small groups are born when the leader consistently seeks and is responsive to the guidance of the Holy Spirit, following His leading throughout the meeting as opposed to sticking to the "agenda." This guidance is especially important during the discussion and ministry time.

Fun!

Dynamic small groups take the time to have fun! Create an atmosphere for fun and be willing to laugh at yourself every now and then!

ABOUT THE AUTHOR

Robert Morris is the lead senior pastor of Gateway Church, a multicampus church in the Dallas/Fort Worth Metroplex. Since it began in 2000, the church has grown to more than 39,000 active members. His television program is aired in over 190 countries, and his radio feature, *Worship & the Word with Pastor Robert,* airs on radio stations across America. He serves as chancellor of The King's University and is the bestselling author of 15 books including *The Blessed Life, Truly Free, Frequency,* and *Beyond Blessed.* Robert and his wife, Debbie, have been married 38 years and are blessed with one married daughter, two married sons, and nine grandchildren. He lives in Dallas, TX.

NOTES

More resources for your small group by Pastor Robert Morris!

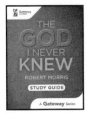

Study Guide: 978-1-945529-54-2
DVD: 978-1-949399-41-7

Study Guide: 978-1-949399-54-7
DVD: 978-1-949399-51-6

Study Guide: 978-1-945529-51-1
DVD: 978-1-949399-49-3

Study Guide: 978-1-945529-71-9
DVD: 978-1-949399-50-9

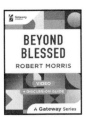

DVD + Discussion Guide:
978-1-949399-68-4

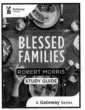

Study Guide: 978-1-949399-55-4
DVD: 978-1-949399-52-3

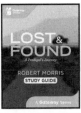

Study Guide: 978-1-945529-85-6
DVD: 978-1-949399-48-6

Study Guide: 978-1-945529-56-6
DVD: 978-1-949399-43-1

Study Guide: 978-1-945529-55-9
DVD: 978-1-949399-42-4

Study Guide: 978-1-945529-88-7
DVD: 978-1-949399-53-0

Study Guide: 978-1-949399-65-3
DVD: 978-1-949399-66-0

Study Guide: 978-0-997429-84-8
DVD: 978-1-949399-46-2

You can find these resources and others at www.gatewaypublishing.com